¡Feliz Navidad!

Celebrating a Mexican Christmas

¡Feliz Navidad!

Celebrating a Mexican Christmas

Christmas Around the World
From World Book

World Book, Inc.
a Scott Fetzer company
Chicago
www.worldbook.com

Staff

Executive Committee
President
  Jim O'Rourke
Vice President and Editor in Chief
  Paul A. Kobasa
Vice President, Finance
  Donald D. Keller
Director, International Sales
  Kristin Norell
Director, Human Resources
  Bev Ecker

Editorial
Manager, Annuals/Series Nonfiction
  Christine Sullivan
Editor, Annuals/Series Nonfiction
  Kendra Muntz
Senior Researcher
  Lynn Durbin
Administrative Assistant
  Ethel Matthews
Manager, Contracts & Compliance
  (Rights & Permissions)
  Loranne K. Shields

Editorial Administration
Senior Manager, Publishing
  Operations
  Timothy Falk

Graphics and Design
Senior Art Director
  Tom Evans
Coordinator, Design Development
  and Production
  Brenda Tropinski
Manager, Cartographic Services
  Wayne K. Pichler
Senior Cartographer
  John M. Rejba

Manufacturing/Production
Manufacturing Manager
  Sandra Johnson
Production/Technology Manager
  Anne Fritzinger
Proofreader
  Nathalie Strassheim

Marketing
Director, Direct Marketing
  Mark R. Willy
Marketing Analyst
  Zofia Kulik
Marketing Specialists
  Anisha Eckert
  Mary Kate House
Digital Marketing Specialist
  Nudrat Zoha

World Book, Inc.
233 North Michigan Avenue, Suite 2000
Chicago, Illinois 60601 U.S.A.

Library of Congress Cataloging-in-Publication Data
¡Feliz Navidad! : celebrating a Mexican Christmas.
     pages cm. -- (Christmas around the world)
     Summary: "A study of the celebrations, customs, and practices of
Mexico and of Mexican Americans. Also includes crafts, recipes, and
carols"--Provided by publisher.
     ISBN 978-0-7166-0830-1
     1. Christmas--Mexico--Juvenile literature. 2. Mexico--Social life and
customs--Juvenile literature. 3. Mexican Americans--Social life and
customs. I. World Book, Inc. II. Series: Christmas around the world.
     GT4987.16.F45 2015
     394.26972--dc23
                              2015023639

Printed in China by Shenzhen Donnelley Printing Co., Ltd.,
Guangdong Province
1st printing September 2015

Table of Contents

¡Feliz Navidad! Celebrating a Mexican Christmas

Introduction

Poinsettias and piñatas, turkey and tamales. Welcome to a Mexican Christmas! Treasured Nativity scenes, called *nacimientos (nah see mee EHN tohs)*, grace homes and churches. On Christmas Eve, a little girl dressed as Mary gently lays an image of the baby Jesus in a manger. Family and friends sing a Spanish lullaby to the Christ Child. Feliz Navidad—Happy Christmas.

Mexican Christmas celebrations have resulted from different people sharing and blending their customs over many centuries. Spanish colonists and missionaries first brought their Christmas customs to Mexico about 500 years ago. Over time, the interaction between the Spanish and the *indigenous* (native) people in Mexico altered some Christmas traditions and started new ones. For example, American foods like corn and chocolate became part of the holiday menu.

A tower of poinsettia plants stands next to a traditional mission-style cathedral at Christmastime in Oaxaca (wah HAH kuh), Mexico.

During a posada celebration, two girls, dressed as the Virgin Mary and her guiding angel, smile and laugh while reenacting the Nativity story.

Mexican traditions have long been part of many Christmas celebrations in areas outside of what is now Mexico. Spain soon expanded its colonial empire to include what is now the southwestern United States. Colonists moved north and northwest from central Mexico, bringing Christmas to this "new Mexico" even before the English colonists founded Jamestown in Virginia or the Pilgrims landed in Massachusetts. Mexican Americans continued many traditions after the region became part of the United States in the 1800's. They also introduced such holiday practices to other parts of the United States. Both American and Mexican traditions have borrowed Christmas customs from the other, continually adapting new ideas into their own existing celebrations.

In the Mexican tradition, the holiday season is both a time of devotion and a joyous fiesta that lasts for many weeks. It's a chance for families and friends to gather, visit, and celebrate—usually with a piñata and crafts for the children. Today in Mexico, children enjoy a long school holiday, and many adults take vacation time to try to keep up with the marathon of parties.

At the heart of the holiday excitement is a series of religious celebrations. They begin on December 16th, with nine days of *posada* processions that reenact Mary and Joseph's journey to Bethlehem. On *Noche Buena* (the Good Night, or Christmas Eve), many families go to church and usually attend a solemn midnight Mass, followed by a dinner feast. In Mexico, a jubilant medley of bells, whistles, and firecrackers welcomes Christmas Day, or *Navidad*.

The festivities in Mexico continue with the Day of the Innocents on December 28 and New Year's Eve on December 31. Children wait for gifts from the Three Kings, also known as the Three Wise Men, given on January 6th. Traditionally, one final celebration on February 2nd—Candlemas— winds up the season.

Used as a decoration for many holidays, colorful pieces of cut paper called papel picado *hang over streets and doorways. With thousands of possible patterns, both children and adults enjoy sharing this traditional folk-art craft.*

Spanish explorers claimed large areas of land that later became part of the United States (see historical map at right). Beginning in the 1500's, the Spanish explored and settled in areas of what are now Mexico; the U.S. states of Florida, Texas, New Mexico, and California; and the Gulf Coast region. Spain lost most of its territory in North America by the early 1800's.

A current map of Mexico shows the terrain and major cities within its boundaries (below). During the 1400's and early 1500's, the Aztec Empire stretched across part of Mexico and Central America (inset, bottom left).

Woven around these special days are all sorts of foods, games, music, theater, and holiday fun. In Mexico, the days are warm and sunny, the nights cool and refreshing. Marketplaces and department stores overflow with toys, candies, and pyramids of fruit. An evening posada procession that once moved through quiet village streets by candlelight now takes place in a busy city beneath trees twinkling with thousands of tiny electric lights. In Los Angeles, California, a similar procession—including people dressed as Joseph, Mary, shepherds, and angels—walks past the shops and cafes of Olvera Street, part of the city's El Pueblo de Los Angeles Historical Monument. Mexican bakeries in places as diverse as Mexico City and Chicago preserve tastes of the season that families just can't do without.

In the modern world, busy families rarely follow all of the traditional holiday methods. Instead, each family selects from the enormous treasury of Mexican holiday customs to create its own very special version of a Mexican Christmas. ¡Feliz Navidad!

In plazas around the world, festive Christmas decorations often adorn the walkways. In the Jardin Zenea (hahr DEEN zeh NAY uh) in Querétaro, Mexico, oversized ornaments, bright poinsettias, and red bows add holiday cheer to the square.

In Mexico City, a massive, artificial Christmas
tree stands next to the Catedral Metropolitana,
the oldest cathedral in Latin America.

Christmas in Colonial Times

The celebration of Christmas came to Mexico in the early 1500's, brought by Spanish explorers and the Roman Catholic missionaries who accompanied them. Early Mexican Christmas celebrations included song, dance, bonfires, fireworks, and lively plays based on the Biblical Christmas story. Some of these elements reflected the efforts of early missionaries to make the message of Christianity meaningful to the indigenous peoples of Mexico. As Spain's colonial territory expanded, the customs established in central Mexico also spread and were further influenced by American Indian groups in new regions, including what is now the southwestern United States. The interaction between Spanish and indigenous cultures became the basis for some of the most treasured Christmas traditions in Mexican culture.

A new faith

Explorers from Spain first set foot on the Mexican coast in 1517. At that time, the Aztec (also called the Mexica—*meh hee cah*) ruled a powerful empire in Mexico. In 1519, the Spanish explorer Hernán Cortés led an army to conquer

Festive lights twinkle in the doorways of El Santuario de Chimayo (chih MY oh) in New Mexico throughout the Christmas season.

A detailed lithograph depicts the first meeting between the Aztec chief Montezuma and Spanish explorer Hernán Cortés.

the Aztec and capture their fantastic treasury of gold. Supported by groups within the empire that wanted to overthrow Aztec rule, Cortés conquered the capital at Tenochtitlan *(tay nohch TEE tlahn)* in 1521 and destroyed the empire. He built a new Spanish capital, now Mexico City, where Tenochtitlan had stood. Mexico soon became a Spanish colony.

Spanish monarchs supported the colonization of North America. One of their goals was to spread the Catholic faith, so they sent missionaries to teach Catholicism. The missionaries tried to find ways to help the Aztec and other Native Americans relate to Christian beliefs and worship.

The Spaniards discovered that the Aztec celebrated the birth of Huitzilopochtli *(WEE tsee loh POHCH tlee)*, their god of the sun and of war, in December near the time of the winter solstice—around the same time as Christmas. The festival celebrating Huitzilopochtli's birth included nights of singing, dancing, and speechmaking. It also included blood sacrifices. The Aztec paraded under flowery arches wearing their finest clothes and adorned with brightly colored feathers. Huge bonfires in courtyards and on the flat roofs of houses lit up the sky for miles around.

The Spanish missionaries took note of the parallels—and the differences—between the two celebrations. In place of the Aztec god of war and the cruel bloody sacrifices associated with his worship, they offered the Christmas promise of divine love and peace given to all people through the birth of the Christ Child. They looked for ways to include the more peaceful Aztec expressions of worship, such as music and pageantry, into the worship practices of Mexico's churches. Pedro de Gante, a monk from Flanders (now Belgium) who arrived in Mexico in 1523, translated songs, including Christmas songs, into *Nahuatl (NAH wah tuhl)*, the Aztec language. The description of an early Christmas celebration that he organized in Mexico City reports that he invited all the indigenous people from nearby. They came in droves, some by land and others by water. Even the sick managed to come, carried in hammocks.

The indigenous people loved the new celebration and adopted it wholeheartedly. So many people assembled at some Christmas Masses that they spilled over into the church courtyards. Bonfires were now lit to celebrate Christmas.

Our Lady of Guadalupe is one of the most powerful Christian symbols that welcomed the peoples of America into the Christian faith. Tradition says that on December 9, 1531, Juan Diego, a recent Mexican convert to Christianity, saw a vision of the Virgin Mary, who spoke to him in Nahuatl. She told him to ask the bishop to build a shrine where she stood on Tepeyac Hill, in what is now Mexico City. The bishop was skeptical, until the vision returned and produced a sign. On December 12, she appeared to Juan and again spoke to him in his own language.

The Aztec used a form of pictograhic writing to learn Bible stories.

Beautiful wooden beams line the ceiling of the Mission San Francisco de la Espada in San Antonio, Texas.

She told him to gather roses from the hill and carry them to the bishop in his *tilma,* a type of long cloak. When Juan unfolded his cloak in front of the bishop, the roses fell out and revealed that an image of the Lady had appeared on the cloak. She later appeared to Juan's uncle and called herself Holy Mary of Guadalupe.

Today, Our Lady of Guadalupe, also called the Virgin of Guadalupe, is the patron saint of Mexico and of the Americas. Roman Catholics celebrate her feast day on December 12. Although not strictly a part of the celebration of Christmas, the day is a national holiday in Mexico near the opening of the holiday season.

Telling the Christmas story

In Europe during the Middle Ages, preachers used religious plays to teach Bible stories to their congregations. Some Spanish missionaries in America also staged such religious dramas in their churches. Performance had also been a part of Aztec religion. Native Americans often participated in Christmas plays

Adorned with long feathers and carrying traditional hand drums, dancers perform around a statue of Our Lady of Guadalupe outside Guadalupe Church in Santa Fe, New Mexico.

La Noche de los Rábanos

When Christmastime draws near in Oaxaca, Mexico, many people look forward to *La Noche de los Rábanos (lah NOH chay deh lohs RAH bah nohs)*, or the Night of the Radishes. Held every year on December 23, this local sculpting competition draws thousands of visitors to the *zócolo (ZOH cho loh)*, or town plaza, to view the beautiful displays of carved radishes. Professional artists, amateur crafters, and children alike spend hours carving intricate designs into the skin of giant radishes grown especially for this event— some more than 2 feet (50 centimeters) long. The competitors have only a few days to carve their entries before the radishes spoil. Their sculptures can vary in shape from small, human figures to entire nacimientos constructed only of radishes. Thousands of people come for the competition and the music, dancing, and fireworks that follow.

This whimsical event originated in the late 1800's when Spanish missionaries introduced radishes to the native peoples. One year, an abundant crop of radishes led the missionaries to bring the root vegetable to the local Christmas market. To attract the attention of shoppers in the marketplace, Oaxacans applied their traditional craft of woodcarving to the vegetable, carving designs on the outside of the radish instead of wood. These radish designs became such a popular local craft that, in 1897, the city of Oaxaca named December 23 the official date of an annual radish carving competition.

Angels and flowers surround a statue of a patron saint, the Virgin of Solitude, all completely carved of radishes, on display for La Noche de los Rábanos.

Hours of work went into carving this single figure of a potter.

by acting, singing, and playing music. Many people wanted to be cast in humorous roles, such as the bumbling and mischievous shepherds, who provide comedic relief for the play. The story of the shepherds' trip to Bethlehem became the subject of boisterous Christmas plays called *pastorelas (pahs toh REH lahs)*. The word *pastor* means *shepherd* in Spanish. The comedic shepherds in these stories had to overcome many obstacles to reach Bethlehem. The theme of these plays is that in the contest between good and evil, good always wins.

In the 1580's, Friar Diego de Soria of the monastery of San Agustín Acolman near Mexico City began celebrating nine Christmastime Masses, one each night from December 16 to December 24. He held the popular services outside in the church courtyard to accommodate large crowds. The practice spread quickly. Sometimes parishioners acted out scenes from the Nativity story. Christmas carols, an organ, hand bells, rattles, and *huijolas (whee HOH lahs*—traditional Aztec whistles) added music. The services might end with fireworks, sparklers, and the breaking of a piñata. In time, the ceremonies moved from the churches to people's houses. They became the basis for the Mexican tradition of *Las Posadas,* a nine-night series of processions reenacting Joseph and Mary's journey to Bethlehem.

Christmas customs spread

By the middle of the 1600's, images and paintings of the Virgin Mary or the Three Kings could be seen in the windows of almost every Mexican house during the holiday season. Some homeowners constructed magnificent altars in front of their houses and hung gorgeous rugs and tapestries from the balconies. The rosary was recited aloud in the streets. People met and mingled in the main squares, enjoying the decorations and visiting busy market stalls.

As Spanish colonial settlement spread throughout the Americas, so did the developing Mexican Christmas customs. The Spanish government established the viceroyalty of New Spain in 1535 to govern most of its northern territories in America. The viceroyalty was centered on what is now Mexico, but eventually expanded to include most of Central America and the Southwestern region of what is now the United States. Spanish missionary priests began religious settlements, called *missions*, where they taught Christian beliefs to various groups of American Indians. Some American Indians lived and worked at the missions. Each mission had a church, workshops, living quarters, and a farm.

Missions and settlers took posadas, pastorelas, and other Christmas traditions to new regions. The first Christian religious drama performed in New Mexico took place in 1598, the year the first Spanish settlement in New Mexico was established at San Juan de Los Caballeros *(cah bah YEHR ohs)*. In the *pueblos* (towns) of New Mexico, American Indians built small bonfires called *luminaries* out of piñon pine logs stacked in three-foot-high squares to light the paths of the posadas. After Mexico gained its independence in 1821 and the region from Texas to California became part of the United States in the mid-1800's, Christmas customs and foods with roots in colonial Mexico remained part of the celebrations in these areas, especially among people of Spanish and Native American heritage.

High on rooftops of the adobe houses at the Taos Pueblo in northern New Mexico, luminaries blaze as people gather to celebrate Christmas.

Las Posadas: A Journey with Mary and Joseph

The Mexican term for Christmas is *la Navidad,* meaning *the Nativity.* Even though the holiday season is a busy, festive time, the true religious meaning of the celebration is not forgotten.

Each December, the Bible's Christmas story comes to life through the Mexican tradition of reenacting Mary and Joseph's journey to Bethlehem on the first Christmas Eve. This family festival is called Las Posadas. This celebration takes place in places as widespread as Acapulco in Mexico; Albuquerque, New Mexico; and New York City.

A little child leads
Traditionally, posadas take place on nine consecutive nights from December 16 to December 24. Las Posadas is based on the

Two teenagers portraying Mary and Joseph lead a group of church parishioners during a Las Posadas processional in Brentwood, California.

Bible's Nativity story in Luke 2:1-7 that tells of Joseph and Mary's long journey from Nazareth and search for lodgings in Bethlehem. The Bible says that when Mary gave birth, she wrapped the baby in swaddling clothes and laid him in the manger of a stable because there was no room for them to stay at the town inn. The Spanish word *posadas* means *inns,* or *lodgings.* Each night's posada reenacts this Nativity story.

Each evening starts with a procession that begins at dusk. A child dressed as an angel often takes the lead. Two people, usually children, who represent Mary and Joseph follow the angel. Sometimes they wear costumes or carry pictures or statues of Mary and Joseph. Groups of children, adults, and possibly musicians round out the procession. Singing or chanting posada songs, they all slowly walk along. Children may carry lighted candles or *faroles,* transparent paper lanterns attached to long poles.

When the procession reaches a house, chosen in advance, the *peregrinos* (pilgrims) sing verses asking for lodging for Mary and Joseph. The people in the house, representing the *hosteleros* (innkeepers), reply in song that they have no room to spare. The pilgrims move on to several more houses, where they sing additional verses asking for lodging and receive more refusals.

Finally, the procession arrives at a house chosen in advance as the "inn." The song explains who the pilgrims are and that Mary will soon give birth to the Son of God. This time, the innkeepers welcome the exhausted travelers by singing, "Enter, holy pilgrims. Come into our humble dwelling and into our hearts. The night is one of joy, for here beneath our roof we shelter the Mother of God."

The innkeepers lead everyone in the procession inside their home to the room containing their *nacimiento* (Nativity scene). If the children playing Mary and Joseph are carrying images, they place them in the nacimiento. Then, the participants may pray, recite the rosary, and sing Christmas carols.

For eight nights, the same events are

Near the end of a posada procession in Albuquerque, New Mexico, the two children dressed as Mary and Joseph are finally welcomed into an "inn" after knocking on several doors asking for lodging.

Children acting as angels carry lanterns to light the way while leading a Christmas Eve posada in Columbia, California.

reenacted, with different children playing the angel, Mary, and Joseph, and the procession winding up at a new "inn" each night. On the ninth evening, Christmas Eve, a particularly impressive posada takes place to welcome the Christ Child. In some communities, Mary carries an image of the baby and lays Him in His crib in the nacimiento. In others, two people designated as the godparents bring the Christ Child to the manger. Traditionally, a Midnight Mass follows the last Christmas Eve posada.

On all nine nights, the solemn religious part of the evening is followed by supper and a party. Food often includes sandwiches, tamales, cookies, and *ponche* (fruit punch), or *champurrado* (a warm spiced drink). After dinner, children break a piñata filled with candy and treats. Many hosts offer each guest a small *aguinaldo* (*ah gwee NAHL doh*—gift) to take home. The aguinaldo is usually a small basket or package containing cookies, fruit, and *colaciónes* (*koh lah see OH nays*—assorted candies).

Four hundred years of tradition

The idea of commemorating the Holy Family's journey to Bethlehem over a period of nine days is traced back to the Spanish religious leader St. Ignatius Loyola. In the mid-1500's, Loyola suggested a Christmas *novena,* special prayers or services to be performed on nine successive days. In 1580, the Spanish religious leader St. John of the Cross made a religious pageant out of the proceedings. The Spanish missionary Friar Diego de Soria formally introduced these observances in America in 1587 in the form of nine outdoor Masses on the nine nights leading up to Christmas Day. At first, these events were solemn and deeply religious in feeling, but they soon became filled with a spirit of fun and excitement. Eventually, the celebrations shifted to people's homes. The posadas became a community affair with friends, relatives, and neighbors gathering together to share the festivities.

Variations in this truly Mexican Christmas celebration have appeared over time and in different regions. Many processions go house to house, but in some cases, they go from room to room within a single home. In modern cities with busy streets, processions may travel through hallways from apartment to apartment. Some families still organize and attend posadas on all nine nights. Other people may only participate in one or two posadas, most often held on Christmas Eve.

Here, there, and everywhere

In the southwestern United States, posadas have remained a living tradition since Spanish colonial days. In sprawling communities, everyone might drive to one host home each night, where they divide into two groups—innkeepers and pilgrims—and sing the verses of the posada song from inside and outside the house. Community groups and churches, including some of the old mission churches, also organize these events. In San Antonio, Texas, the Hispanic Heritage Society sponsors La Gran Posada. One evening each December, a huge posada progresses through the heart of the city to San Fernando Cathedral.

Mexican Americans also have introduced posadas in communities farther north, although weather conditions in cities like Chicago, New York, and Toronto have inspired some posadas to move indoors for this traditionally outdoor event. December weather in New York, for example, can bring rain, sleet, snow, or temperatures well below freezing.

Other congregations with large Mexican American memberships may organize an outdoor procession that ends at the church because the number of participants is too large for a family home. Families share responsibility for providing food at the church. The guitars, cornets, and violins of a local mariachi group may play *villancicos* (*vee yahn SEE kohs*—Mexican Christmas songs) interspersed with American carols while children swing a baseball bat at a piñata.

Las Posadas is one of the favorite and most enduring Mexican Christmas traditions. Whether the children playing Mary and Joseph wear sandals or snow boots, it has remained a treasured family practice for many Mexicans and people of Mexican heritage.

A painting titled Mexican Posada Procession in Chicago (below) by Franklin McMahon shows that cold and snowy winter weather does not deter community posada festivities.

Nacimientos — Little Towns of Bethlehem

The Spanish phrase *el nacimiento* means *the birth*. A nacimiento is a miniature scene that represents the birth of Christ in Bethlehem. In some parts of the world, it is called a *crèche (kresh)*, a manger scene, or a Nativity scene. Regardless of its name, the scene often includes a stable and always the figures of Mary, Joseph, and baby Jesus. It also may include such other figures as the shepherds, their animals, and the Wise Men who visited the Christ Child.

The family

In the Mexican cultural tradition, the nacimiento has been the main Christmas decoration in family homes. It is the center of family devotion and activity during the Christmas season. Nacimientos also appear in such locations as churches, plazas, parks, and store windows.

The traditional day for decorating and setting up nacimiento displays is the 16th of December, the day the first posada begins. However, today families set up their displays at various times

Wooden nacimientos are popular at community centers, department stores, and nongovernmental outdoor spaces in both Mexico and the U.S. This nacimiento is displayed at the Olvera Street Bandstand in Los Angeles, California.

before Christmas Day. As families unpack their tucked-away boxes of nacimiento figures, everyone has their favorite pieces. Cherished figures tend to get passed down from generation to generation.

Families often set up the nacimiento on a table or in the corner of a room. Mary, Joseph, and a manger to hold the baby Jesus always fill the center of the scene. Angels hover above, and shepherds approach the stable. However, the manger remains empty until the baby is placed in it on Christmas Eve, the night when the birth of Jesus is celebrated. Similarly, the figures of the Three Kings are traditionally added on January 6, when the church calendar commemorates their visit to the Christ Child.

The not-so-little towns

A nacimiento may be anything from a simple grouping of the Holy Family to the entire countryside of Bethlehem, populated by a dozens of people and animals. Large, grandiose Nativity scenes—some taking up an entire room—are well-known in Mexico, but much less common in the United States. In Mexico, some people put their nacimiento in an open doorway or window so it is visible to neighbors passing by.

Small nacimientos of painted ceramics are traditional Mexican Christmas decorations. Different regions of Mexico favor different colors and styles for such traditional folk-art figures as these.

Scenes change from year to year. Boxes draped with cloth or paper represent hills or mountains. Moss and artificial grass provide lush greenery. A winding road of white sand may lead from the top of a mountain down to a cluster of tiny houses forming the town of Bethlehem. A mirror can represent a pond, or a clever builder might engineer a tiny flowing waterfall. Flowers cover the hillsides, which may also have a dusting of powdery snow. Cut-out stars or cotton clouds may dot a dark backdrop. Above it all, the Star of Bethlehem shines down.

The next step is to add Mary, Joseph, and the manger to the center of the scene. Hay may be placed in the manger awaiting the child's arrival. In Mexico, people often populate their nativity scenes with dozens of additional figures from all sorts of times and places. Tiny figurines portray villagers going about their everyday tasks in and around Bethlehem from 2,000 years ago. Figures may include such distinctively Mexican characters as a taco seller, a balloon vendor, or a person making tamales. Off to the side might be a little scene from Noah's Ark or a monk kneeling before a crucifix. Horses, donkeys, dogs, camels, and chickens can also make an appearance. A rooster may call from a rooftop. According to Mexican folklore, a rooster flew up to a high perch and crowed to announce the Christ Child's birth. Soon, other roosters took up the cry to spread the good news.

A ceramic Arbol de Vida (Tree of Life) candelabra shows a Nativity scene in the center.

Nacimientos tend to grow year by year, as families find new figures at stores and marketplaces to add to their arrangements. Each year, collectors watch for new pieces in their favorite styles.

The artists

Designers produce beautiful figures for nacimientos out of glass, lead, plastic, pottery, silver, wax, and even cardboard. Folk

artists craft delicate figures from cornhusks, dried flowers, wheat straw, and woven reeds.

Many art museums have added nacimientos made by Mexican and Mexican American artists to their folk art collections. The Panduro family of Tlaquepaque, a suburb of Guadalajara, produces outstanding ceramic manger scenes with intriguingly realistic figures. Galardón Pantaleón Panduro, born in the mid-1800's, was known as *El Brujo* (the wizard) because his skill seemed to make the clay speak. The family's artistic tradition is still carried on by Panduro's great- and great-great-grandchildren. Four sisters from the Aguilar family in the Oaxaca region and their mother, artist Doña Isaura Alcántara, are members of another family known for distinctive ceramics, including nacimientos. The town of Metepec west of Mexico City is renowned for a unique type of polychrome ceramic called *Arbol de la Vida,* or *Tree of Life,* depicting generations of people from Biblical history. The special Christmas Tree of Life has a Nativity scene in the center.

The history

The custom of setting up a manger scene at Christmas can be traced back to the Italian friar St. Francis of Assisi. In 1223, he told a friend that he wanted to celebrate Christmas by creating a Nativity scene with a live donkey and ox as a reminder of Christ's humble birth.

From Italy, the custom traveled to Spain and then Mexico. At first, the scenes generally included only the three main figures of Joseph, Mary, and Jesus, and were called *misterios* (*mih STEH ree ohs*—mysteries). The central part of all nacimientos today is still referred to by that name. In Mexico, craftspeople began to shape the figures from a lightweight wood that is easy to carve. They might cover the sculptures with a thin coat of plaster or silver and paint them with brilliant colors. Nuns in convents or daughters of the household sewed beautiful costumes to place on the figurines. The custom spread quickly. Soon every household in Mexico, rich or poor, had its own Nativity scene at Christmastime. The nacimiento has remained central to Mexican Christmas traditions everywhere.

El Nacimiento

The Tucson Museum of Art and Historic Block includes La Casa Cordova, one of the oldest extant adobe structures in downtown Tucson, Arizona. The Museum displays a permanent installation, *El Nacimiento*, an elaborate arrangement of hundreds of miniature figures that illustrate scenes from the Bible, as they might have occurred in a Mexican village.

Such depictions include a market, a kitchen with cooks, and small replicas of fruits, vegetables, kitchen utensils, and furniture. Prickly pear cacti are shown in the yards of the country dwellings. Children love to search for items in the display, which contains surprising additions to traditional nativity narratives, such as holiday lights and swans.

Angels hung from the ceiling of El Nacimiento *soar above a waterfall flowing down a mountainside, in this rural scene of a woman washing clothing.*

Prickly pear cacti line the front of this Mexican casa (house) scene depicting daily village life.

Starting in 1978, Mexican folk artist Maria Luisa Tena spent months of each year preparing and arranging the Nacimiento display in memory of her mother. Over the years, the Nacimiento grew in size and complexity, and incorporated more elaborate buildings, scenes, and hundreds of figures. In 2008, *El Nacimiento* was permanently installed in the historic La Casa Cordova at the Museum.

El Nacimiento is a permanent installation in the historic La Casa Cordova at the Tucson Museum of Art and Historic Block in Arizona.

La Noche Buena — The Holy Night

La Noche Buena, the Good, or Holy Night, is Christmas Eve. In Mexican culture, it is the peak of the holiday celebrations each December. It is an evening for solemn religious remembrance of the birth of the Christ Child. It is also a special time for family, food, and fun.

In most homes, the manger in the family's nacimiento has been empty until now. Traditionally, a young girl in the family receives the honor of placing the baby Jesus in the manger this evening. Among families that participate in a Christmas Eve posada, the girl playing Mary may put the baby Jesus in the manger of the nacimiento at the end of the posada. Then, everyone sings a Christmas lullaby to the child.

Some towns or churches hold special Christmas Eve processions, called *candelas*. In the city of Oaxaca, Mexico, the posadas end at neighborhood churches. Then, the candelas leave the churches

Glistening gold pillars, red holiday bows, and pretty poinsettias decorate the Metropolitan Cathedral Basilica in Mexico City for Christmas Eve Mass.

In Mexico's Yucatán Peninsula, families light candles and carry religious banners while participating in one of many Christmas Eve candelas processions.

and crisscross the city as they head for the town's main plaza. Groups carry lanterns and religious banners. Decorated cars and trucks, transformed for the night into religious floats, join the parade, as do giant puppet-like figures on stilts. The groups circle the plaza and then return to their own churches for midnight Mass.

The Mexican tradition of attending a midnight church service on Christmas Eve dates back to colonial times. The Spanish missionaries sent to America were Roman Catholic, and the majority of Mexicans and Mexican Americans are still Roman Catholic today. The traditional Catholic midnight Mass on this night is called the *Misa de Gallo* (Rooster's Mass) because a Mexican legend tells of a rooster crowing the announcement of the Christ Child's birth. Throughout Mexico, church bells ring after the Mass and fireworks light up the sky.

A late-night supper follows church, so families return home to the smell of delicious foods that likely have been cooking all day. As in many cultures, holiday foods are among the most enduring traditions. Often the main dish is roast turkey. *Ensalada de Noche*

Buena (Christmas Eve salad) contains apples and other fruits, beets, lettuce, and nuts. Additional favorite dishes include fish, *romeritos* (greens similar to spinach), and tamales. *Buñuelos* (thin, crispy, deep-fried dough, sprinkled with sugar and cinnamon) are a traditional Christmas season desert. Ponche, *atole* (a holiday drink made of corn meal spiced with cinnamon), or hot chocolate with vanilla and cinnamon may top off the meal. After the late Christmas Eve dinner, children look forward to breaking piñatas and, maybe, some presents.

The celebration on Christmas Eve continues well past midnight. Since children (and adults) were up late, Christmas Day is a generally a quiet time in Mexico. In the U.S., kids may be sent to bed earlier on Christmas Eve in anticipation of opening gifts from Santa the next morning. In Mexican culture, some people may attend Mass on Christmas Day, held in the morning and at noon. Families and friends may cook *pozole*—a stew made with corn meal, meat, and vegetables—using the leftovers from the previous night. *Feliz Navidad* (Happy Christmas) greets each newcomer who comes to call.

The main dish of Christmas Eve dinner is usually a roast turkey.

Red Chile Ristras

An iconic representation of the state of New Mexico, red *chile ristras* are strings of dried red chilies that hang near windows, balconies, and archways through the fall and winter months. Thought to bring good health and good luck, ristras are a communal sign of welcome and are especially common decorations during such holidays as Christmas and New Year's. The dried chilies are not only decorations—they are often used to cook favorite dishes and sauces for various celebrations throughout the holiday season.

The annual chile crop is grown in the spring and summer months. In the fall, the vegetable ripens on the plant and changes color from green to dark red.

Red chile ristra strings are used in a variety of ways including as a decoration, as a sign of peace, or as an ingredient in a favorite holiday dish.

Once it turns, the chilies are harvested and strung on a line to dry outdoors in the hot sun. This useful preservation method allows for the chilies to be rehydrated and eaten in the cold winter months.

Ristras are often handmade. Some families carry on the tradition of making their own red chilie ristras at home, but ristras are also readily available for purchase at Christmas markets. Typically, ristras are made out of dozens of red chilies and heavy twine. The chilies are grouped in bundles and the twine is tied around the chile pod stems. This action is repeated many times. As more chilies are tied, the string becomes longer and longer. The traditional shape of ristras hang vertically about 3 feet (1 meter) long, but they can be made in a variety of sizes and shapes, such as stars and wreaths.

In Santa Fe, New Mexico, a woman demonstrates to a young child how to tie red chilies by hand to form a ristra string.

Maybe a gift or two?

The long-time Mexican tradition of giving gifts to children on Three Kings Day, January 6, came from Spain. On that day, the Roman Catholic Church commemorates the Epiphany, the visit of the Three Kings who brought gifts to the Christ Child.

In the colonial United States, by contrast, immigrants from many different places brought with them a whole variety of gift-giving traditions. People of Spanish heritage gave children gifts on Three Kings Day. Dutch children received gifts on St. Nicholas's Day (December 6). British and German immigrants gave gifts on Christmas Day. Only in the 1800's did gift-giving on December 25 become the main American tradition.

Today, Mexican Americans generally give children gifts on Christmas Eve or Day. The custom began drifting south into Mexico during the 1900's. Many children in Mexico now receive a few gifts at both Christmas and Three Kings Day. Often, those received at Christmas are opened following the late-night Christmas Eve dinner. In some families, the tradition is to say the gifts at Christmas are from the Christ Child. Other families, particularly in urban areas, credit the presents to a visit from Santa Claus.

Pancho Claus, a Tex-Mex version of Santa Claus, is credited for bringing children gifts at Christmas in many Texas cities in the United States. Pancho Claus was created during the Chicano movement, a civil rights campaign started by Mexican Americans in the 1960's.

¡Feliz Navidad! Celebrating a Mexican Christmas

Tamales, Poinsettias, and Shared Traditions

The cultural sharing that began when Spanish and American Indian customs first met has continued to influence Mexican holiday traditions to the present day. Many Mexican Christmas traditions come from Old Spain. Others, like decorating with poinsettias, began in Mexico and have been embraced throughout the world. The interchange continues today, as some Mexicans adopt new traditions—such as the Christmas tree—and people in other places add a bit of Mexican color and sparkle to their celebrations.

A food with American roots

A number of Mexican holiday foods, such as the special cake called *Rosca de Reyes* eaten on Three Kings Day, reflect a Spanish influence. Other favorites, such as tamales, have roots in the land's precolonial past. Corn, also called *maize,* is native to the Americas. A tamale consists of *masa,* a corn meal dough, that is spread onto a cornhusk. A

Christmas lights and ristra strings decorate amber adobe buildings in Santa Fe, New Mexico, while a large nutcracker soldier stands watch.

filling—typically of meat, beans, and vegetables—is spooned on top of the dough, then the whole bundle is rolled up, sealed, and steamed. The cornhusk wrapping is discarded before eating. The name *tamale* comes from the Aztec word *tamalli,* meaning *carefully wrapped.* However, tamales existed thousands of years before the Aztec culture began. Hunters and warriors from such earlier Mexican cultures as the Olmec, Maya, and Toltec carried tamales with them when they traveled.

Making tamales is time-consuming work. It was once common for the women and girls in Mexican and Mexican American families to gather for a *tamalada* (tamale-making party) to make tamales for the Christmas season. Some families still manage to carry on the tradition. A tamalada can even be a sort of family reunion. But all too often in these busy times, homemade tamales from the kitchen of a grandmother or a special aunt exist onlu as a fond childhood memory for those in both the U.S. and Mexico.

Christmas theater, Mexican style

First introduced in Mexico by missionaries in the 1500's, *pastorelas* were plays about the journey of the shepherds to Bethlehem. They were a way to teach the Christmas story to people who were not able to read the Bible themselves. Since then, generations of performers in the Americas have added their own cultural stamp to the productions.

In the Bible story, angels appear to the shepherds to tell them the good news of the birth of the Messiah, and the shepherds arrive at the stable in Bethlehem without incident. In the *pastorelas,* however, the shepherds encounter a whole series of wild and crazy setbacks as Lucifer tries unsuccessfully to disrupt their journey.

Mexican hot chocolate

A popular ingredient in a wide variety of sauces, desserts, and beverages, chocolate can play a large role in the holiday season. Mexican hot chocolate is an especially popular drink on La Noche Buena. Cacao beans, from which chocolate is made, are native to the Americas. The Maya and Aztec made cold, bitter-tasting beverages from ground cacao nibs (peeled cacao beans), water, and spices. Later, Spanish missionaries were introduced to cacao beans in Mexico and brought the ingredient back to Europe. When recreating the chocolate drink, Europeans replaced the water with warm milk and added sugar, creating a sweet version of hot chocolate that is still consumed around the world today.

Modern Mexican hot chocolate contains a special type of dark chocolate and a mixture of such spices as nutmeg, allspice, vanilla, and chilies. The chocolate used in this drink is made of roasted cacao nibs that are stone-ground and combined with cinnamon, sugar, and, sometimes, cocoa butter. Usually, this chocolate combination is granular in texture and is packaged as flat disks of solid chocolate. Extra spices can be added to the ground cocoa nibs before packaging, creating a solid, spiced chocolate bar. The solid chocolate is then broken off in small increments to melt into the warm milk beverage. Frothy hot chocolate is common in Mexico and is made today by whipping the warm mixture with a whisk or a *molinillo*—a special wooden mixer that is rolled back and forth between the palms. Once foamy, the drink can be served with a cinnamon stick or topped with whipped cream.

Molinillo
(moh lih NEE yoh)

Cacao beans were once used as both an ingredient and currency in the Aztec community. An Aztec sculpture from the 1500's depicts a man holding an oversized cacao bean.

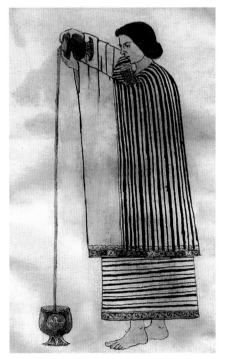

A painting from about 1550 shows an Aztec preparing a chocolate drink—creating froth by rapidly pouring the mixture between drinking vessels.

The last act of the play always sees the beleaguered shepherds finally reach the manger in Bethlehem and present the Infant Jesus with gifts. The Virgin Mary blesses them and, usually, everyone dances and sings as the curtain falls.

For generation after generation, amateur groups performed the *pastorelas*, often handing down the words by memory and adding new plot twists and comedy gags. The attitudes and humor of the performers became a large part of the plays.

During the 1800's, small groups of players from rural areas of the American Southwest toured during the holiday season. Each group performed its own version of a *pastorela* for audiences in towns or out on big ranches. Their homemade masks and costumes often revealed the influence of the region's Native American art. In the late 1800's, small professional companies from Mexico that toured north of the Rio Grande helped establish a tradition of Spanish-language theater in Texas.

Groups interested in folk theater continue to hold *pastorela* performances each December in both Mexico and the southwestern United States. New elements in today's performances often include jokes about politicians and comments on social issues.

Christmas legends of flowers and vines

An old Mexican legend tells of a poor child who wanted more than anything to visit the manger in the village church. (In some versions of the legend, the child is a boy; in others it is a girl.) The child was sad because she had no gift to bring to the tiny Christ Child. Along the way, she noticed a bush growing beside the dusty road. She thought she could at least take a few of its green branches to present to the newborn Babe.

Miraculously, some of the leaves turned scarlet and blossomed in the shape of brilliant red stars. The girl had a lovely gift for the Infant Jesus. When she laid the branches at the foot of the crib, the Virgin Mother raised her hand in a gesture of love. Outside in the velvety dark sky, a bright star appeared in the east and shone down in splendor over the little Mexican village. Mexicans call the plant *flor de Noche Buena,* meaning *flower of the Holy Night* or the *Christmas Eve flower.* This legend led Mexicans to decorate with poinsettias at Christmastime.

La flor de Noche Buena blossoms high above the rooftops in Mexico City.

Poinsettias are native to Mexico and Central America. The wild plants can grow up to 15 feet (4.5 meters) high. The Aztecs used the plant to make red dye and to treat fevers. Poinsettias have tiny yellow flowers surrounded by large colored *bracts* (special leaves) that resemble flower petals. The bracts turn color, usually red, when the days grow shorter in the fall. During colonial times, people noticed that poinsettias changed color just before Christmas, so they associated the star-shaped red display with the legend and the birth of Christ. They began using the plants to decorate their Nativity scenes.

In 1825, Joel Robert Poinsett, the first American ambassador to Mexico and an

Shops throughout Mexico, such as this one in Playa del Carmen (seen below), sell popular tin ornaments to adorn Christmas trees. The tin ornaments come in a wide variety of shapes and sizes and are painted with bright colors that stand out against a green tree (above).

amateur botanist, admired the plants and sent cuttings home
to his greenhouse in South Carolina. Later, he gave samples to
several botanist friends. In the English language, the plant became
known as the poinsettia, named after Poinsett. It became a popular
Christmas decoration in the United States and many other
countries during the 1900's.

A somewhat similar legend is told in Texas about a plant called
the *Márgil* vine. Adina de Zavala recorded the story and other
legends as part her work to preserve the history of Spanish culture
in Texas. She was the granddaughter of Lorenzo de Zavala, who
had served as the first vice president of the independent Republic
of Texas in 1836.

In the early 1700's, the missionary Friar Antonio Márgil visited
the Mission San Antonio de Valero (better known today as the
Alamo) in what is now San Antonio, Texas. The padres had placed

*In rural areas, finding
a robust cut Christmas
tree is difficult for
many families. The
solution—decorating
a living tree outdoors.*

a nacimiento in the church, and the Indians living nearby brought small gifts to adorn it.

The legend says that Márgil saw a small boy crying outside the church and asked the boy why he was upset. The boy said he had no gift to give the baby Jesus. "Give him your heart and your service," said the friar, but the boy wanted a gift that he could see.

Márgil sent the boy home for a jar, then helped him dig up a little vine with dark green berries and plant it in the jar. "It's not very beautiful," said the boy, but Márgil told him the Christ Child would make it pretty. The boy placed the jar next to the manger and promised to loyally serve the Christ Child in the years to come. Suddenly, the plant's leaves glistened and the berries turned a bright ruby color. The boy was overjoyed. The Christ Child had made his gift a beautiful offering.

Christmas trees and Santa Claus

Compared to some other Mexican holiday traditions, Christmas trees are a relatively recent addition. The custom of putting up Christmas trees began in Germany in the 1500's. German royalty brought the idea to England when they married into the British royal family. When Americans and Canadians saw prints of the British royals around a Christmas tree, the custom became popular in North America in the mid-1800's. Today, Americans of virtually all ethnic groups have made Christmas trees a part of their holiday tradition. Mexican Americans often place their nacimiento on a table next to the tree. In some regions, it is also customary to place a picture of the Virgin of Guadalupe nearby.

Christmas trees have become popular in Mexico since the mid-1900's. Some people with large nacimientos have been known to incorporate their tree right into the Nativity scene. Favorite tree decorations in Mexico include strings of tiny lights, tinsel, Spanish moss, and many types of ornaments, especially tin. Towns often set up a large tree in the central plaza.

The Christmastime legend of Santa Claus also became popular in the United States during the 1800's. For Dutch colonists, the symbol of gift giving was Saint Nicholas, whom they called *Sinterklaas*. Among English-speaking children, that name eventually became *Santa Claus*. Poems, stories, and magazine

illustrations from the 1800's and early 1900's shaped the modern image of Santa as a stout, jolly man who drove a sleigh pulled by reindeer and delivered presents on Christmas Eve. During that time, Santa gradually became the main symbol of gift giving for most Americans, including Mexican Americans. Today, like most of American society, Mexican American parents worry about the commercialism that has become associated with the symbol.

Santa's popularity spread to Mexico in the late 1900's. In Mexico today, old and new traditions exist together. Before Christmas, parents may take little children to see both Santa Claus and the Three Kings to pose for pictures and ask for gifts.

Children look forward to visiting with Santa Claus each year to ask for gifts and pose for pictures in Mexico City.

Piñatas

Piñatas are a Mexican cultural tradition that has become popular in the United States. In Mexico, piñatas have played a role in Christmas celebrations since Spanish missionaries in the 1500's made them part of church festivals, including Christmas Eve.

Christmastime piñatas come in a dazzling array of colors and shapes—burros and flowers, stars and cartoon characters. Before a party, the piñata is filled with as much candy, nuts, fruit,

Making a piñata takes patience and creativity. Initially, piñatas were made with a decorated clay pots filled with goodies. Today, some piñatas still contain a clay pot at the center, but most are made of colorful papier-mâché and filled with candy, fruit, or small toys.

and small toys as it will hold. Then the host strings the piñata to be pulled up by a rope, with one end of the rope free to allow the piñata to move up and down.

The game begins when the host blindfolds a would-be piñata breaker, hands him or her a big stick, and twirls the player around and around. The now-dizzy competitor tries as hard as possible to strike the piñata—but it's not where it was a second ago. The person in charge of the rope busily raises and lowers the piñata, always trying to keep it out of reach of the flailing stick. Finally, a player connects. The piñata breaks, spilling its treasures, and everyone scrambles to share in the treats.

Some traditions give the Italian traveler Marco Polo credit for bringing the piñata from China to Italy around the year 1300. Chinese piñatas were fashioned in animal shapes. They were filled with seeds and served as part of New Year's festivities.

In Italy, the piñata was a fragile clay pot called a *pignatta* (which means *fragile pot*). Guests at masquerade balls broke pineapple-shaped pignattas filled with sweets. The game became associated with the religious season of Lent, which occurs before Easter each spring. This event found its way to Spain, where the first Sunday of Lent became known as Piñata Sunday.

Brought to Mexico by missionaries in the 1500's, the piñata was quickly accepted by the Aztecs, who had a very similar custom. Toward the end of each year, the Aztec priests prepared an offering for Huitzilopochtli, their god of war. On a pole in the temple, they placed a clay pot filled with small treasures and covered it with finely woven feathers. The pot was broken with a club, and the gifts tumbled down at the feet of the idol.

The Spanish word *piñata* originally referred to the game. The container itself was called an *olla* and was, as in the Italian version, left undecorated. Before long, however, people began to dress up the homely pot. In Spain, a seven-pointed star became the traditional shape for piñatas. According to one explanation, the seven points represent the seven deadly sins. The blindfold symbolized faith, a willingness to trust in things unseen, and the stick was the believer's fight against evil. When the piñata broke, the treats represented God's blessings, which rained down on everyone. Later, people in Mexico began to associate the star piñatas at Christmas celebrations with the Star of Bethlehem.

Piñatas eventually became a part of many Mexican festivals, both religious and nonreligious, and the custom soon spread to the United States. In the mid-1900's, Mexican American craftspeople in the southwestern United States became known for creating extravagant handmade piñatas.

Today, children around the world look forward to breaking piñatas to celebrate birthdays, national holidays, and other special events. Some piñatas still have a clay pot at their center, but more often they are made of papier-mâché. Sometimes they are fashioned to look like cartoon characters or superheroes. The widespread popularity of the piñata has crossed into many cultural groups who incorporate the use of piñatas into their own celebrations.

Children collect candy after breaking a star-shaped piñata, a symbol for the Star of Bethlehem.

¡Feliz Navidad! Celebrating a Mexican Christmas

Wishes for the New Year

Traditionally, Mexican holiday celebrations go on past Christmas Day. In Mexico, children eagerly await the arrival of gifts from the Three Kings on January 6, but two other days of fun and parties come first.

Mamá, may I borrow your phone?

December 28 is *el Día de los Inocentes,* the Day of the Innocents. It's sort of an April Fools' Day in December, when children look forward to playing tricks on their friends and relatives. In Mexico, the favorite trick is to try and fool people by borrowing money or some small, treasured object from them. Later on, the trickster "innocently" tries to return a little toy or something absolutely worthless instead. Of course, it's all in good fun. (Mamá will get her phone back...eventually.)

Booming fireworks light up the night sky at midnight on New Year's Eve in Acapulco, Mexico.

The history of this day began with the remembrance of a sad biblical event. The Bible says that when the Wise Men told King Herod about the star that signaled the birth of a Jewish king, the Messiah, Herod was afraid of losing his throne. He ordered his soldiers to kill all the infant boys in Bethlehem. Joseph and Mary managed to escape from Bethlehem with their child. On the Day of the Innocents, the church commemorates the innocent children that Herod ordered killed. In Spain, their spirit of fun and spontaneity eventually turned the day into one of such children's games as hide-and-seek and "find the hidden object." In Mexico, playing pranks on el Día de los Inocentes grew from this Spanish legacy.

At the stroke of midnight, such church bells as those at the Santa Prisca Cathedral in Taxco, Mexico, ring in the new year.

New Year's Eve wishes

New Year's Eve is a time for parties and lots of noise. In Mexico, children stay up late and join the fun. At the stroke of midnight, church bells ring out, drivers honk their horns, firecrackers go off, and fireworks burst into the air. Families often share a late New Year's Eve dinner of pork or turkey, perhaps accompanied by lentil soup.

The welcoming of the new year is a time to think about renewal and wishes. As in most cultures, it is also a day for all sorts of quirky customs and superstitions. One Mexican custom is to eat 12 grapes at midnight, one with each chime of the church

bells, to sweeten the 12 months of the coming year with good luck. Some versions of the custom say to make a wish on each grape—12 wishes!

Another custom directs those who wish to take a trip in the new year to take an empty suitcase for a walk around the house, or around the block, depending on the distance of the travel destination. Another option is to find a broom and sweep the old year out the door at midnight. Some people throw coins on the porch and sweep them back into the house for prosperity. If one really wishes for money in the coming year, they wear green underwear on New Year's Eve. Wearing yellow underwear is said to bring good luck, red brings love, and white brings peace.

Music and parties are a popular part of New Year's Eve celebrations for people from just about all cultural backgrounds in Mexico and the U.S. In both countries, New Year's Day is a national holiday and a good chance to rest after late night parties.

Many customs are linked to the beginning of a New Year. For some, it is a chance to literally sweep away the past year by taking a broom and sweeping debris out of the front door (below left). For others, hanging such items as balloons with the colors of yellow, red, or white can bring luck, love, and peace, respectively, in the New Year (below right).

Celebrations at the Close of the Season

After the New Year's celebrations, there are two more festivities that round out the holiday season. The first, Three Kings Day, is a time for gift giving on January 6th. Then, on Februray 2, Candlemas is the last event celebrated as part of the Christmas season.

Three Kings Day

On the evening of January 5, children all over Mexico fidget and fuss and try to be good. That night, the Three Kings will journey past the children's homes, leaving gifts of toys and candies.

The Three Kings are also known as the Three Wise Men. The Bible tells how they followed a star, searching for the child who had been born King of the Jews—the Messiah, Jesus. At last, they found

A unique sight in Puerto Vallarta, Mexico—sculptures, such as these of the Three Kings, made entirely from sand.

"the child with Mary his mother; and they knelt down and paid him homage. Then, opening their treasure chests, they offered him gifts of gold, frankincense, and myrrh" (Matthew 2:11).

For centuries, Roman Catholic and Protestant churches have celebrated the visit of the Three Kings on January 6, the feast day of Epiphany. In Mexico, the day is called *el Día de los Reyes Magos*—the Day of the Kings, or Three Kings Day. Traditionally, it is a day for giving gifts to children, just as the Three Kings gave gifts to the baby Jesus.

In many parts of the country, each child expectantly sets a pair of shoes out on a balcony or windowsill on the evening of January 5. Some children fill the shoes with hay—a snack for the camels that the Three Kings ride. They might even slip in a letter to the Kings asking for a special present. The next morning, the hay and letters are gone, replaced with a pile of candy, nuts, and toys. Even though many children also receive presents at Christmas, Three Kings Day is still the main gift-giving day in Mexico.

In Canada and the United States, Christmas generally

Three Kings Day parades occur in many urban areas through the United States and Mexico. In Brooklyn, New York, elaborately costumed folk dancers dress as each of the Three Kings.

has become the main time for presents, although some Hispanic families attempt to keep a tie with the Spanish/Mexican tradition by also giving children one or more small gifts on January 6. However, one Three Kings Day custom remains a big favorite. The *Rosca de Reyes,* or Three Kings Cake, is a ring-shaped coffee cake with candied fruit on top. The cake looks like a crown with jewels on it. Hidden inside the cake is a small plastic or porcelain token representing the baby Jesus. The hidden image symbolizes how Joseph and Mary had to hide the infant Jesus from Herod.

Mexican bakeries in U.S. cities with large Mexican American populations are busy in the days leading up to January 6. They produce the cakes in all sizes for families, neighborhood parties, church groups, and businesses.

Towns in Mexico often arrange to serve a big Three Kings Cake to the public. In Mexico City, more than 2,000 bakers combine their talents to bake and assemble a gigantic Rosca de Reyes in the zócalo, the city's central square. They use tons of butter, flour, and sugar and about 40,000 eggs to create a ring-shaped cake that, if opened out, would measure about 1 mile (1.6 kilometers) long or more. About 200,000 people come to enjoy a slice.

On el Día de los Reyes Magos, a long-time family custom is for each person to cut his or her own piece of cake. The person who gets the piece with the baby inside is the lucky one selected to

A Three Kings Day celebration in Mexico City includes city officials simultaneously cutting into an enormous Rosca de Reyes, or Three Kings Cake, to share with the community members gathered at the zócalo. The historic Catedral Metropolitana can be seen in the background.

host a party on February 2, the church feast day called *el Día de la Candelaria*. In some stores and businesses, employees share a Three Kings Cake. The person who finds the image of the baby may bring a treat—maybe donuts and coffee—for coworkers on February 2.

Candlemas

After Three Kings Day, life begins to quiet down again in Mexico. It's been nearly a month of religious festivals and processions, parties and piñatas. Even before the first posada, there was the excitement of the national holiday celebrating Our Lady of Guadalupe, the country's patron saint, on December 12. Recently, Mexicans now fondly refer to the whole extraordinarily busy, festive period from December 12 to January 6 as Guadalupe-Reyes or the Guadalupe-Reyes Marathon.

These days, most Mexican and Mexican American families pack away their nacimientos and other Christmas decorations on or shortly after Three Kings Day, but some people wait until February. In the traditional church calendar, the final Christmas-related festival falls on February 2. *El Día de la Candelaria,* called Candlemas in English, commemorates the presentation, according to Jewish custom, of the baby Jesus at the temple in Jerusalem 40 days after his birth. The Biblical story says that the prophets Simeon and Anna recognized the baby as the Messiah who would be the light of the world. In keeping with this theme, people traditionally bring candles to the church to be blessed on this day. Following an old Mexican tradition, some families bring their image of the Christ Child to church on Candlemas to be blessed by the parish priest. This is also the day to gather for dinner or a snack at the home of the "host" who found the tiny token of the Holy Child in his or her piece of Three Kings Cake a month ago. The practice is no longer as widespread as it once was, but some families and friends still get together for a light supper—perhaps tamales and hot chocolate.

Candelaria is mainly a religious and family celebration, but some Mexican towns welcome the chance for fireworks or a festival. Tlacotalpan *(tlah ko TAHL pahn),* a charming city in the Mexican state of Veracruz near the Gulf of Mexico, holds a Candelaria festival that lasts several days. A procession carries an image of the

A group of women hold dressed-up dolls to represent the Christ Child during a Mexican Candelaria festival.

Christ Child from the local church through the graceful arches and brightly painted colors of the town's beautifully preserved colonial buildings to the Papaloapan River. There, the procession continues on the water as a parade of boats.

With the passing of el Día de la Candelaria, one more Christmas season becomes a memory, another year in the centuries-long history of Mexican Christmas traditions. The holiday customs of the past and the present continue to flourish in Mexico and among people of Mexican American heritage. Cherished nacimiento figures, passed down through the family, may stir memories of midnight Mass in a village church for people who have moved to a big city. Parents remember the taste of the tamales at grandmother's house in Guadalajara, Veracruz, or maybe Los Angeles. Meanwhile, children eagerly look forward to the posadas and piñatas, the flavors and fun of continuing the Christmas traditions next year—and maybe starting some new ones!

Crafts

Poinsettia

What you will need:

- red construction paper
- ruler
- pencil
- scissors
- glue
- pumpkin seeds
- red spray paint
- white peppercorns
- red yarn

1. Cut a 2 ¼-inch (5.75-cm) circle out of red construction paper. (The bottom of a small juice glass can be used to trace the circle.)

2. Glue the outer row of pumpkin seeds to the construction paper in a circular pattern. The pointed end of the seeds for all rows should be facing the center of the circle.

3. For the second row, place a dot of glue on a pumpkin seed and position the seed on top of the outer row, in between two seeds. Repeat this step until the second circle is complete.

4. Repeat this process used for the second row to fill the third and final row. Let dry completely.

5. Spray the front with red spray paint. When dry, turn over and spray the back.

6. To add the hanger, cut a length of yarn about 9 inches (23 cm) long and glue to the back of the poinsettia. Out of the construction paper, cut out a circle about 1 ¾ inches (4.5 cm) and glue over the yarn to hide the ends and to secure. Let dry.

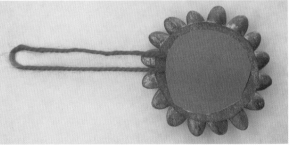

7. Turn over and glue 8 to 9 white peppercorns in the center. Until the glue sets, the peppercorns might slip a little. If so, use the tip of the pencil to reposition them.

Lamb piñata

Although the star is a traditional shape, piñatas can depict almost anything, like the little lamb that accompanied the shepherds visiting the Christ Child in the manger. Making this lamb requires several days to accommodate drying times.

1. Inflate a balloon to about 30 inches (76 cm) in diameter and knot the end. Tie a piece of string to the knotted end and hang the balloon at a comfortable working height. Wherever you choose to work, be sure the surfaces can easily be wiped down because applying paste-soaked newspaper strips can be messy. Lay newspaper sheets below the balloon.

2. Draw an oval no larger than 3 inches (7.6 cm) wide, about 2 ½ inches (5.5 cm) from the top. This area will be the opening used to fill the piñata with treats.

3. Dip a newspaper strip into the paste, wipe off the excess between your thumb and forefinger, and lay onto the hanging balloon in a vertical direction. Continue laying down strips until the balloon is completely covered. Do not cover the opening drawn in Step 2. (Continued on page 66.)

What you will need:

- one 12-inch (30.5-cm) round white balloon; should be able to inflate to 30 inches (76 cm) in diameter
- newspaper, torn into 2-inch (5-cm) strips*
- paste made from one part flour and two parts water**
- stiff felt, black and white
- one roll of white crepe streamer, 1 ¾ inches x 175 feet (4.5 cm x 53 m)
- an awl or similar pointed tool
- bowl   • string   • marker
- ruler   • scissors   • white glue

*Do not cut paper; torn strips will adhere better.
**1 cup flour and 2 cups water was used to make this lamb, but you may use a bit more or less depending on the size of the balloon. Note, excess paste should not be disposed of in a sink for it may clog pipes. Discard excess paste in a garbage container.

4. Repeat step 3, but alternate the direction in which you apply the strips. In the end, you will have a total of four layers, (vertical, horizontal, vertical, horizontal). These layers give the piñata strength. Apply four layers of newspaper strips. Allow to dry about three days. Note, the top will dry faster than the bottom. If the bottom begins to sag during the drying process, remove the balloon from the hanging position and invert it in a bowl.

5. When thoroughly dry, deflate balloon. It will fall away from the newspaper shell and can be discarded.

6. Using a bowl for a stand, rest the newspaper shell on top. With an awl,

make two holes, about 2 inches (5 cm) from the top on either side of the 3-inch (7.6-cm) opening. Thread a string approximately 30 inches (76 cm) long through the holes and knot. Pull the string up, and now you have a hanger for your piñata.

7. Enlarge the pattern at the bottom of this page 200%. Cut the face, inside circles of eyes, and four legs out of the black felt. Cut the outer circles of the eyes and mouth out of the white felt. Glue the eyes and mouth to the face.

Enlarge 200%

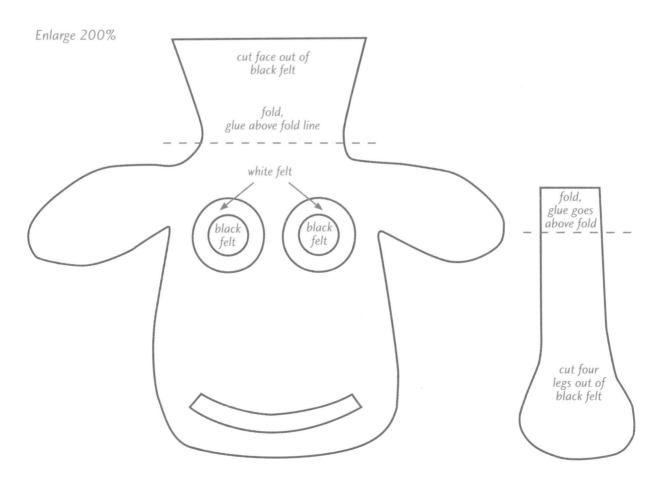

cut face out of black felt

fold, glue above fold line

white felt

black felt *black felt*

fold, glue goes above fold

cut four legs out of black felt

8. Glue only the top part the face and front legs onto the shell as shown. The face will act like a flapped hinged cover for the opening of the shell and the legs should dangle. Allow the glue to dry.

9. Turn the shell over and glue the top part of the hind legs as shown. The bottom of the legs will dangle. Let the glue dry.

10. Prepare the crepe streamer fringe for the lamb's coat in sections. Cut a length of streamer, fold it in half, and then fold the length into 6-inch (15.25-cm) sections, accordion style. Fringe the section by cutting from the open edge to within ¼ inch (0.6 cm) of the fold. These slashes should be about ⅛ inch (0.3 cm) apart.

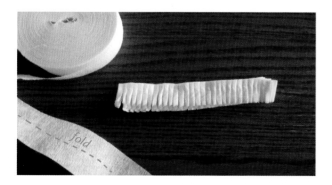

11. Using a bowl for a stand, position the newspaper shell head-side down in the bowl. Working in concentric circles, begin gluing the fringe. The fold side should face the head and the fringe should slightly overlap the preceding row so that only fringe is visible.

12. Continue applying the fringe until the shell is completely covered. The fringe should go under the legs and head and over the glued flap. Hang by the string handle and let dry completely.

13. Lift the head and fill with wrapped candy or small toys and hang from a high area.

Ojo de Dios

The ojo de Dios (God's eye) has been made by the Indians of Mexico and Central America for hundreds of years. The diamond pattern is the symbol of the eye of God. The bands of color around the central diamond are said to symbolize the wisdom and light coming from the eye.

What you will need:
- popsicle sticks
- 3 to 5 vibrant colors of yarn
- scissors
- ruler

1. Make a cross with two popsicle sticks. Choose a color yarn that will be the middle of the eye and begin wrapping the yarn around the intersection of the sticks to form an "X." Try to keep the sticks centered on each other. Wrap around at least four times in each direction to secure. Tie a knot and trim off the loose end.

2. Start winding the yarn around the crossed sticks by wrapping the yarn around a stick, giving the cross a quarter turn, and wrapping around the next stick. Keep repeating this wrap around and quarter-turn technique, following the "X" shape made in step 1. As you wrap and turn, keep the yarn taut.

3. To change colors, tie the next color yarn onto the previous color. Position the knot next to a stick. Wind the yarn several times around the stick to hide the ends and continue the wrap/ quarter turn process.

4. When you get to about $^3/_8$ inch (1 cm) from the end of the sticks, stop winding. Pull a loop of yarn through the last wrap to make a hanger as shown. Turn over and knot the ends. To secure the hanger, turn over and tie another knot on the back side. Cut the single strand of yarn at the knot.

5. To make the bows, loop a length of yarn so that there are four loops approximately 2 inches (5 cm) long. Take another long length of yarn and tie in the middle, as shown at right.

6. Tie the bow tightly to the front of a yarn-wrapped stick, overlapping the last few rows of yarn. Wrap the ends around the stick two to three times and knot. Trim the excess yarn. Repeat this step for the remaining three sticks.

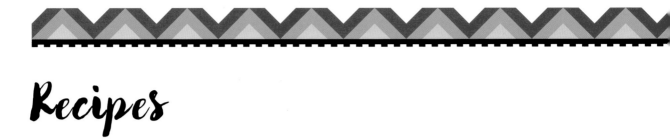

Recipes

Pozole   8 to 10 servings

2 pork hocks, each split into two or three pieces
1 large onion, sliced
2 cloves garlic, minced
Water
1 stewing chicken, cut into serving pieces
1 pound pork loin, boneless, cut into 1-inch chunks
2 cups canned hominy or canned garbanzos
1 teaspoon salt
$\frac{1}{2}$ teaspoon pepper
1 cup radishes, sliced
1 cup cabbage, shredded
1 cup lettuce, shredded
$\frac{1}{2}$ cup green onions, chopped
1 avocado, diced
Lime wedges

1. Put the split pork hocks, onion, and garlic into a large pot or Dutch oven. Cover with water, and cook on the stove on a medium heat until almost tender, about 3 hours.
2. Then, add chicken and pork loin to the pot and cook 45 minutes, or until chicken is almost tender.
3. Add hominy, salt, and pepper. Cook about 15 minutes more.
4. Remove pork hocks and chicken from soup. Remove meat from bones and return meat to soup. Continue heating until soup is warmed through.
5. Serve in large soup bowls. Accompany with a relish tray offering radishes, cabbage, lettuce, green onions, avocado, and lime wedges as garnish.

Empanadas   around 30 empanadas

Filling:

½ pound beef, coarsely chopped
½ pound pork, coarsely chopped
½ cup onion, diced
1 small clove garlic, minced
½ cup raw apple, diced
¾ cup tomatoes, diced

¼ cup raisins
¾ teaspoon salt
⅛ teaspoon pepper
Dash ground cinnamon
Dash ground cloves
¼ cup almonds, chopped

Pastry :

4 cups all-purpose flour
1 ¼ teaspoons salt

1 ⅓ cups lard or shortening
⅔ cup ice-cold water

1. For filling, cook beef and pork together in large skillet until well browned. Add onion and garlic and cook until onion is soft. Add remaining ingredients, except almonds, and simmer 15 to 20 minutes.
2. Stir in almonds. Cool.
3. For pastry, mix flour and salt in a bowl. Cut in lard until mixture resembles coarse crumbs. Sprinkle cold water over flour mixture, stirring lightly with a fork until all dry ingredients hold together. Divide dough in 4 portions.

4. On a lightly floured surface, roll one portion of dough at a time to ⅛-inch (0.3-cm) thickness.
5. Cut 5-inch (13-cm) rounds of pastry with a knife. (Use a bowl to cut around as a guide.) Place a rounded spoonful of filling in the center of each round. Fold and seal each round by dampening inside edges of pastry with water and pressing together with the tines of a fork.
6. Place empanadas on a baking sheet. Bake at 400 °F (204 °C) for 15 to 20 minutes, or until lightly browned. Or, fry in deep-frying oil heated to 365 °F (185 °C) until browned, about 3 minutes, turning once.

Sweet Tamales   3 ½ dozen tamales

3 ½ dozen large dry corn husks
1 cup lard (or ½ cup lard and
 ½ cup butter)
1 cup sugar
4 cups dehydrated masa flour (*masa harina*)

1 teaspoon salt
2 ½ to 3 cups warm water or fruit juice
Date-pecan filling (or other fruit or
 nut filling of your choice)

Sweet Tamales:

1. Wash corn husks in warm water. Place in pan and cover with boiling water. Let soak at least 30 minutes before using.
2. Beat lard until light and fluffy, using whisk or electric mixer.
3. Combine masa flour, sugar, and salt. Gradually beat this mixture and water into lard until dough sticks together and has a paste-like consistency.

4. Shake excess water from each softened corn husk and pat dry on paper towels. Spread about 2 tablespoons tamale dough on center portion of husk, leaving at least a 2-inch (5-cm) margin at both ends and about ½-inch (1.25-cm) margin at right side. Spoon 1 ½ tablespoons filling onto dough. Wrap tamale, overlapping left side first, then right side slightly over left. Fold bottom up and top down. If husks are too short to stay closed, they may be tied with string or thin strips of corn husk.
5. Lay tamales in top section of a steamer with open flaps on bottom. Tamales may completely fill top section of steamer but should be placed so there are spaces between them for circulation of steam.
6. Steam tamales over simmering water about 1 hour, or until corn husks can be easily peeled from dough.

Date-Pecan Filling:

Blend 1 cup brown sugar, ¼ cup butter or margarine, and ½ teaspoon cinnamon until smooth. Add 1 cup chopped, pitted dates and 1 cup chopped pecans. Toss until evenly mixed.

Red Snapper Veracruz Style

About 6 servings

1/4 cup olive oil
1 cup onion, diced
1 clove garlic, minced
2 cups (16-ounce can) diced tomatoes,
  with liquid
1 teaspoon salt
1/4 teaspoon pepper
2 pounds red snapper fillets
1/4 cup pimento-stuffed olives
2 tablespoons capers
Lemon wedges

1. Heat oil in a large skillet. Cook onion and garlic in oil until onion is soft, about
   5 minutes. Add tomatoes, salt, and pepper and cook about 5 minutes to blend
   flavors; slightly chop tomatoes as they cook.
2. Arrange red snapper fillets in a 3-quart baking dish. Pour sauce over fish.
   Sprinkle with olives and capers.
3. Bake in a preheated 350 °F (175 °C) oven for 25 to 30 minutes, or until fish can be
   easily flaked with a fork. Serve with lemon wedges.

Nut Cookies

About 4 dozen cookies

1 cup butter or margarine
3/4 cup confectioner's sugar
2 cups all-purpose flour, sifted
3/4 cup nuts, chopped

1. Beat butter until creamy. Add sugar, mixing
   until light and fluffy.
2. Stir in flour and nuts. Mix well.
3. Shape into 1-inch (2.5-cm) balls. Place onto
   greased baking sheets.
4. Bake in a preheated 350 °F (175 °C) oven for 12 to 15 minutes.
5. Remove from oven while still warm.
6. Roll cookies in additional confectioner's sugar. Cool completely on wire rack.

Torrejas de Coco French toast served at posadas   About 12 servings

4 cups sugar	1 (1 ½-pound) loaf	1 cup lard	¼ cup pine nuts or
1 ½ cups water	egg bread, sliced	1 cinnamon stick	chopped almonds
2 cups shredded	3 eggs	3 tablespoons raisins	
coconut	1 tablespoon flour		

1. Dissolve 1 cup of sugar in ½ cup of water in a saucepan over medium heat. Bring to boiling; boil 3 minutes. Add shredded coconut. Let it cook until the moisture is absorbed and coconut becomes a dry paste, about 15 minutes. Remove from heat and cool slightly.
2. Spread some coconut paste between two slices of egg bread, forming a sandwich.
3. Beat eggs with flour. Dip both sides of sandwich in egg mixture and fry in butter in a skillet, about 1 minute on each side. Drain on absorbent paper. Repeat with additional bread slices.
4. Make a syrup by combining 3 cups of sugar, cinnamon stick, and 1 cup of water in a large skillet. Heat 5 minutes. Add browned sandwiches and simmer several minutes, turning once.
5. Remove the sandwiches and arrange on a serving dish. Pour strained syrup over the top and garnish with raisins and toasted pine nuts or almonds.

Chestnut Cake   Makes 2 cakes

1 cup butter	1 teaspoon baking	½ cup milk
1 ¼ cups sugar	powder	½ teaspoon vanilla
6 eggs, separated	1 ¼ cups all-purpose	1 ½ cups chestnuts,
½ teaspoon salt	flour, sifted	chopped

1. Cream butter and sugar until light and fluffy.
2. Add egg yolks one at a time, beating well after each addition.
3. Sift together salt, baking powder, and flour. Add sifted dry ingredients alternately with milk.
4. Stir in vanilla and nuts.
5. Beat egg whites until stiff. Gently fold into cake batter.

6. Pour batter into 2 well-greased and floured 9-inch (23-cm) cake pans.
7. Bake in a preheated 350 °F (175 °C) oven for 30 to 35 minutes.

Apricot-filled Pastries

2 dozen filled pastries

1 cup dried apricots
1 cup water
¹⁄₂ cup sugar
¹⁄₂ teaspoon vanilla extract
2 cups all-purpose flour
³⁄₄ teaspoon salt
¹⁄₂ teaspoon baking powder
³⁄₄ cup lard
4 to 6 tablespoons ice-cold water
Confectioner's Sugar Glaze, optional

1. Put apricots and water into saucepan. Cover, bring to a boil, and cook 20 minutes.
2. Place contents of saucepan into an electric blender. Cover and blend until smooth.
3. Combine blended apricots and sugar in saucepan. Cook until thick, about 5 minutes. Cool slightly and stir in vanilla extract.
4. Mix flour, salt, and baking powder in a bowl. Cut in lard until crumbly. Add cold water, 1 tablespoon at a time, tossing with a fork until dough holds together. Divide dough in half.
5. Roll each half of dough to a 14 x 10-inch (35.5 x 25.5-cm) rectangle on a lightly floured surface.
6. Line a nonstick baking sheet with one rectangle of dough. Spread apricot mixture evenly over dough. Place remaining dough on top, sealing the edges. Poke small holes into the top of the crust.
7. Bake in a preheated 400 °F (205 °C) oven for 25 minutes, or until lightly browned around edges.
8. Cool slightly and frost with Confectioner's Sugar Glaze. Cut in squares after completely cooled.

Confectioner's Sugar Glaze:
Combine 1 cup confectioner's sugar and ¹⁄₂ teaspoon vanilla extract. Stir in about 3 tablespoons of milk or cream until glaze is of spreading consistency.

Buñuelos

2 dozen buñuelos

4 cups all-purpose flour
2 tablespoons sugar
1 teaspoon baking powder
1 teaspoon salt
2 room temperature eggs, well beaten
$^3/_4$ to 1 cup milk
$^1/_4$ cup butter, melted
Oil for deep frying, heated to 350 °F (175 °C)
Granulated sugar-cinnamon mixture
   for dusting

1. Mix flour with sugar, baking powder, and salt in a bowl.
2. Combine beaten eggs and milk. Stir into dry ingredients to make a stiff dough. Add more milk if needed to moisten all dry ingredients. Stir in butter or margarine.
3. Turn dough onto a lightly floured surface and knead 1 to 2 minutes until smooth. Divide dough into 24 balls, or buñuelos. Roll each buñuelo into a round shape about 6 inches (15.25 cm) in diameter.
4. Fry each buñuelo in hot oil until delicately browned, turning once. Drain on absorbent paper toweling. Sprinkle with sugar-cinnamon mixture while still warm.

Candied Pumpkin

l pumpkin (about 6 $^1/_2$ pounds)
4 $^1/_2$ cups firmly packed brown sugar
1 cup water
2 oranges, juice and shredded peel
1 $^3/_4$ cups nuts, chopped

1. Peel skin from, remove seedy center, and shred the fleshy part of the pumpkin.
2. Combine brown sugar and water in a large saucepan. Heat on medium high until sugar dissolves and syrup starts to thicken.
3. Reduce heat to medium low. Add pumpkin to syrup and cook slowly, stirring constantly, for about 10 to 15 minutes.
4. When thickened, add orange juice and shredded orange peel. Continue cooking until thickened, then add nuts.
5. Put candied pumpkin mixture into a baking pan. Let cool about 3 hours. Cut into squares.

Capirotada
6 servings

2 cups firmly packed dark brown sugar
l quart water
1 stick cinnamon
1 clove
6 slices toast, cubed
3 apples, pared, cored, and diced
1 cup raisins
1 cup blanched almonds, chopped
1/2 pound Monterey Jack or similar cheese, cubed

1. Put brown sugar, water, cinnamon, and clove into a saucepan and bring to a boil. Reduce heat and simmer until a light syrup is formed. Discard spices and set syrup aside.
2. Meanwhile, arrange a layer of toast cubes in a buttered casserole dish. Cover with a layer of apples, raisins, almonds, and cheese. Repeat until all ingredients are used. Pour syrup over the top.
3. Bake in a preheated 350 °F oven for about 30 minutes.
4. Serve hot.

Hot Mexican Eggnog
About 7 cups

1 quart milk
8 egg yolks
1/2 cup sugar

1 1/2 teaspoons shredded orange peel
1 1/2 cups brandy or cognac (optional)
Ground cinnamon

1. Scald milk.
2. Mix egg yolks and sugar in a bowl. Add scalded milk gradually, stirring constantly. Pour into top of a large double boiler. Cook over boiling water, stirring constantly until mixture coats the back of a spoon.
3. Remove from water. Add orange peel and brandy (if used).
4. Mix a small amount at a time in an electric blender, or with a molinillo whisk, until foamy.
5. Serve hot. Sprinkle the top with cinnamon.

Songs

This Is the Night

Rather fast (♩. = 80)

And so this is the night of the search for a lodg-ing where Jo-seph and Mar-y can rest. They're so wear-y and foot-sore but no doors are o-pen to those who so soon will be blest. O-pen your doors, o-pen your hearts, So that heav-en can en-ter with-in, so that heav-en can en-ter with-in, so that heav-en can en-ter with-in.

Asking for a Lodging

(JOSEPH) O - pen these por - tals, I pray, for the love of heav - en.

O - pen your heart for a poor wom - an waits out - side.

Wea - ry from trav - el, we seek here a place to rest.

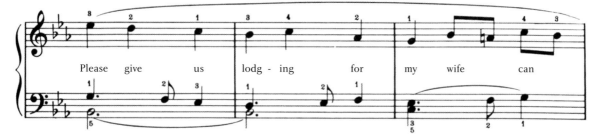

Please give us lodg - ing for my wife can

no long - er ride.

Acknowledgments

Cover:	© Mark Newman, Getty Images
1	© Shutterstock
2-3	© Dreamstime
5	© Shutterstock
6-7	© iStockphoto
8	© Robert Fried, Alamy Images
9	© Shutterstock
10	WORLD BOOK maps
11	© Scott Goodno, Alamy Images
12-16	© Shutterstock
17	© Shutterstock; Public domain image
18	© Mark Kane, Santa Fe Convention and Visitors Bureau
19	© Danita Delimont Stock Photography/Alamy Images; © Jennifer Booher, Alamy Images
21	© Danny Lehman, Corbis Images
22-24	© ZUMA Press/Alamy Images
25	Leslie Davis, Columbia California Chamber of Commerce
27	© Franklin McMahon, Corbis Images
28-29	© Shutterstock
30	WORLD BOOK photo by Christine Sullivan
31	© Oleksiy Maksymenko Photography/Alamy Images
33-35	Courtesy the Tucson Museum of Art
36-37	© iStockphoto
38	© Martin Norris Travel Photography/Alamy Images
39	© Shutterstock
40	© Mark Kane, Santa Fe Convention and Visitors Bureau; © Shutterstock
41	© Eric Gay, AP Photo
42-43	© Steve Hamblin, Alamy Images
44	© Jupiter Images/Getty Images
45	© Shutterstock; Museum Collection Fund, Brooklyn Museum; Public domain image (from the Codex Tudela, Museo de América, Madrid, Spain)
46	© Nik Wheeler, Alamy Images
47	© iStockphoto
48	WORLD BOOK photo by Matt Carrington; © Shutterstock
49	© Russell Monk, Masterfile
51	© SuperStock
52	© Marco Ugarte, AP Photo
53-56	© iStockphoto
57	© Ethan Welty, Aurora Photos/Alamy Images; © iStockphoto
58	© Danita Delimont Stock Photography/Alamy Images
60	© Richard Levine, Alamy Images
61	© Eduardo Verdugo, AP Photo
63	© Edgard Garrido, Reuters/Landov
64-69	WORLD BOOK photos by Brenda Tropinski
70-72	© Shutterstock
73	© Dreamstime; © Shutterstock
74-77	© Shutterstock